Whatever the Weather

Learn about the Sun, Wind and Rain

Written by Steve Parker and Jen Metcalf

Illustrated by Caroline Attia

LITTLE
GESTALTEN

Contents

Weather is everywhere!

Summer, fall, winter, spring: every season has a different type of weather. But the weather also changes from day to day, hour to hour, and minute to minute. Weather is not limited to a single town, country, or continent. No matter where you live, the weather is happening right outside. This book contains lots of cool facts and fun surprises about what happens in our atmosphere—whatever the weather!

How can I find out what the weather will be like tomorrow?

Let's ask the people who know what it will be like!

Woof! Humans spend a lot of time talking about the weather!

Weather can be fun, scary, good, or bad. It's a bit like ice cream flavors: different people like different types of weather. What's your favorite?

Maybe you love snow but hate being too hot in the summer. Some people think thunder is exciting, but others find it frightening. Rain can be annoying, but it's fun to splash around in puddles.

We don't have any control over the weather. Even if you wish really hard for a snowy day, you might only get rain all week.

The best thing to do when you're planning something outside is keep an eye on the weather forecast. That way, you won't end up heading to the beach when it's too cold, or taking a sledding trip when it's too warm.

What can I learn from the sky?

I wonder why some clouds bring snow?

What does a rain cloud look like?

Do any snowflakes look the same?

Look up at the sky

What do you see? Nothing?
Never! There's always something
to see—even if it's just blue sky.

You might see a rainbow!

Sunlight is not only white, it
consists of different colors,
like blue, red, or yellow.
When a sunray hits the
atmosphere (the air around
our Earth) we only see the
blue part of the light. This is
why the sky is blue!

We experience weather with our senses.
You can see the wind shaking trees in
the fall, feel the Sun warming your skin
in the summer, and hear the rain pitter-
pattering on a lake in spring.

Here are some things you might see when you look up: bright sunshine, heavy rain, falling snow, leaves blowing in the wind.

Even if the weather stays the same for several days, eventually it always changes. So if you look up often, you will see just how different the weather can be.

Lightning can heat the air around it to 50,000°F (28,000 °C). That's five times hotter than the surface of the Sun!

Extreme weather can cause a lot of problems. Storms, floods, droughts, and heat waves are dangerous for the people and animals who live in the areas where they happen.

Hooray for summer!

School's out—and so is the Sun! When the Sun is shining in the summer, you can play outside, go swimming, and eat ice cream. It's a lot of fun. Just remember to cover up and spend time in the shade so you don't get sunburnt.

The Sun gives us heat, but did you know that it also powers our weather? By warming the air in some places but not others, it creates wind. Wind drives changes in the weather.

Cloudless blue skies are common in the summer. During the day there's not much wind. This kind of weather is caused by high air pressure, which we'll talk about later.

The Sun's diameter is 110 times larger than the Earth's — similar to the difference between an exercise ball and a cherry!

The ocean absorbs heat during the summer and releases it in the winter. This also affects the weather.

Water heats up much more slowly than land. Have you ever noticed how hot the sand can get when you're heading into the ocean for a cooling dip?

Some places in the world are extremely hot and dry all the time, not just in the summer.

These regions are called deserts. Deserts are so dry because it almost never rains where they are. The Sun is very strong and harsh in these areas, and the ground is made up mostly of bare rocks or shifting sands.

Have you ever looked into the distance on a hot day and seen a pool of water on the street that you know isn't there? That's called a mirage.

It happens when sunlight travels down through cold air and into warm air near the ground. The change in air temperature bends the light and tricks your brain into seeing something that isn't there.

Very occasionally, water does come out of the ground in the desert. It forms a water hole that allows plants and trees to grow nearby. This is called an oasis.

Most plants and animals cannot survive in the desert because of the lack of food and water. For some species, though, the desert is their home. Just think of cactuses and camels!

The Lut Desert in Iran might be the hottest place in the world. In 2005, the temperature there reached 159°F (70°C)!

Snakes and scorpions also live in the desert. They stay cool by burrowing into the sand.

Tropical rainforests are also very hot places.

The Sun can be very bright there, but they are not at all like deserts. This is because the air is very humid, or damp— and it rains a lot. It rains so much because of all the trees and plants. When it rains, the leaves high up in the canopy layer catch a lot of the water. Some rain also reaches the soil on the forest floor and the roots of the trees and plants soak up that water. Then the leaves release some of the water back into the air as water vapor. When this water vapor cools, it forms rain clouds, and the cycle continues.

Rainforests stay warm all year. Temperatures stay mostly between 70 and 85°F (21 and 30°C), even at night.

The canopy layer is way up high. Trees grow really fast to reach this height because it's the best place in the rainforest for sunlight. Sloths and orangutans can be found among the branches.

Trees in the rainforest often have very tall trunks. They have roots, called buttress roots, which stop them from falling over and help them to absorb lots of nutrients from the ground.

One part of the rainforest is neither warm nor sunny: the forest floor is cool and dark because the thick canopy layer stops the sunlight from getting through.

The highs and lows of weather

Air pressure is the weight of the air pressing on everything around. When air rises and falls, it changes the air pressure at the Earth's surface—and this changes the weather.

High pressure usually results in sunshine, clear skies, and calm weather.

This is how it works: Cold air is heavier than warm air. When it sinks downward, the pressure at the Earth's surface rises and this creates a high-pressure area.

Blue is cold air.

Red is warm air.

In a high-pressure area, the air flows down and then out.

Low pressure gives us clouds, wind, rain, and sometimes storms.

Warm air is lighter than cold air. When warm air rises toward the sky, the pressure at the Earth's surface sinks. This creates a low-pressure area.

A barometer is an instrument that measures air pressure. Barometers help scientists to predict the weather.

In a low-pressure area, the air flows up.

Like fireworks but better!

Auroras are amazing natural-light displays that happen way up high, where the air pressure is really, really low. They occur around the north and south poles. The best time to see these colorful ribbons of light is at night—which is strange, because they are actually caused by the Sun!

Auroras that happen at the north pole are called aurora borealis (the northern lights). And auroras that happen at the south pole are called aurora australis (the southern lights).

The Sun is always sending out tiny particles that fly toward Earth. This is known as solar wind. The particles usually just bounce off our planet's magnetic field.

But sometimes the solar wind becomes a solar storm: the particles have so much energy that they crash through the magnetic field and start colliding with gases in our atmosphere.

Which colors you get tosee in the nighttime sky depend on which gases the particles bump into.

Currents put the motion in the ocean!

Seas and oceans have a huge effect on our weather. Warm–water currents carry the Sun's heat to cold places. Cold–water currents carry cool temperatures to hot places. This stops temperatures on Earth from becoming too extreme—and makes our planet a much friendlier home for humans, plants, and animals!

NORTH AMERICA

... up the east coast of the United States and Canada ...

... the Gulf Stream flows past Florida ...

... which becomes the North Equatorial Current ...

Currents are patterns of moving water. They are driven by the wind, the rotation of the Earth, and the temperature and saltiness of the water. Here you can see the Gulf Stream, a current that starts in the Gulf of Mexico. It carries warm water from the Americas across the Atlantic Ocean to Europe and North Africa.

SOUTH AMERICA

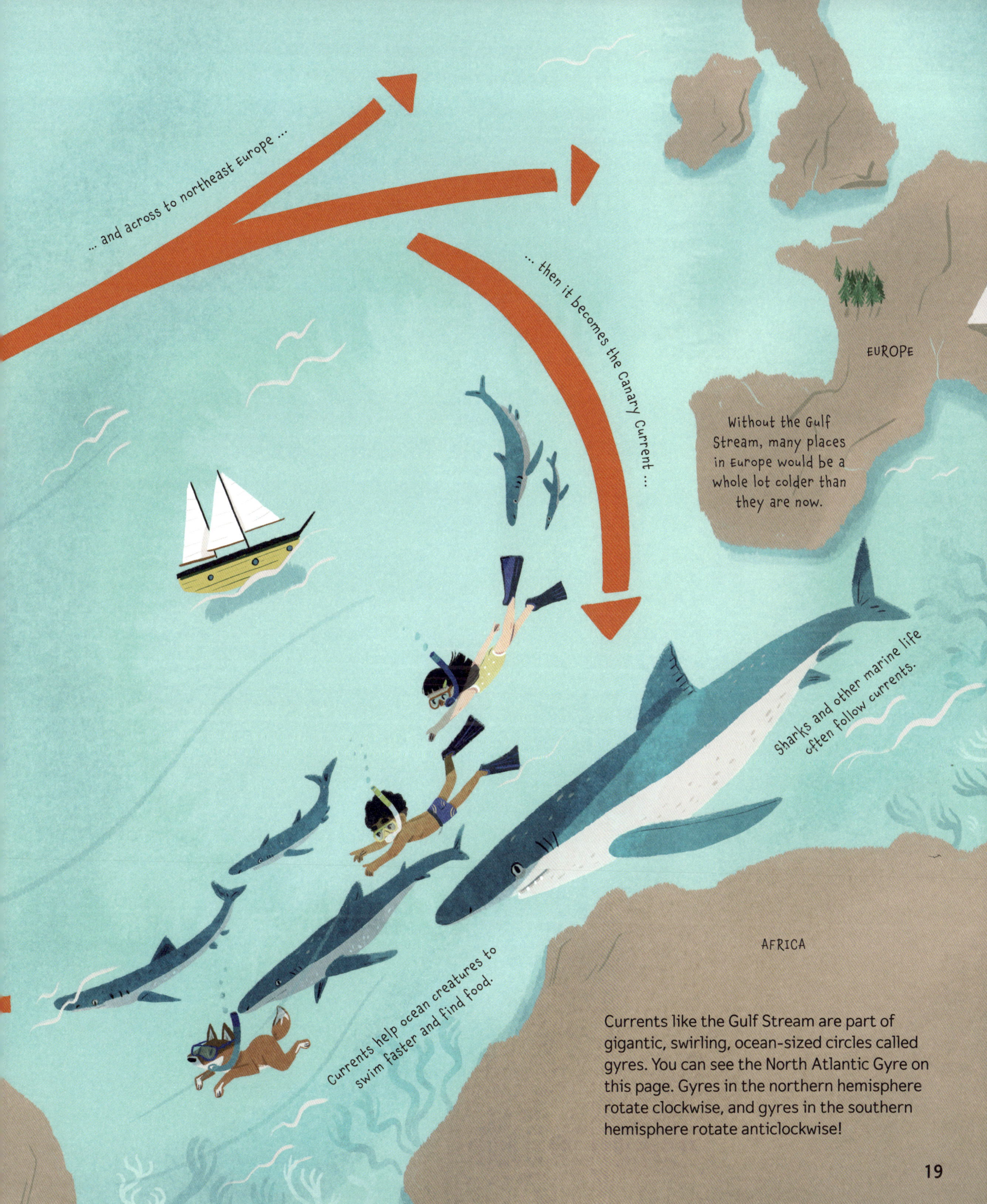

... and across to northeast Europe ...

... then it becomes the Canary Current ...

EUROPE

Without the Gulf Stream, many places in Europe would be a whole lot colder than they are now.

Sharks and other marine life often follow currents.

Currents help ocean creatures to swim faster and find food.

AFRICA

Currents like the Gulf Stream are part of gigantic, swirling, ocean-sized circles called gyres. You can see the North Atlantic Gyre on this page. Gyres in the northern hemisphere rotate clockwise, and gyres in the southern hemisphere rotate anticlockwise!

Fall brings the wind

In the fall, the days become cooler, the leaves change color, and the wind really starts to blow. Like other weather, wind is powered by the Sun. If you get caught in strong wind, it can sometimes feel like you're about to fly away!

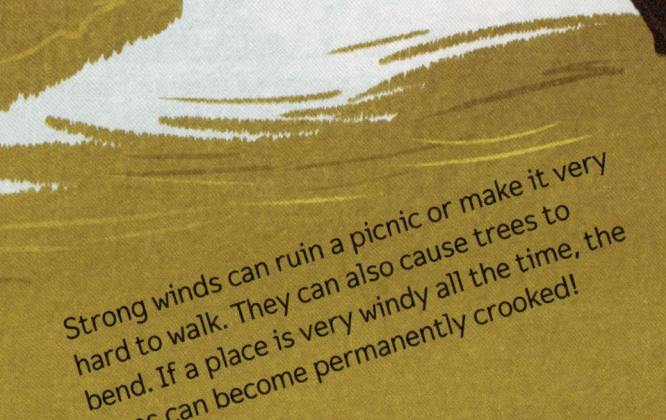

You can tell which direction the wind is blowing by looking at the trees.

Strong winds can ruin a picnic or make it very hard to walk. They can also cause trees to bend. If a place is very windy all the time, the trees can become permanently crooked!

Do you remember high air pressure and low air pressure? They create wind and storms.

When the Sun heats the Earth, it also heats the air. This warm air rises and creates an area of low pressure at the surface below. The missing air mass is replaced by cold, higher-pressure air, from nearby. This movement of air is the wind.

Windy days in fall can get chilly, so wrap up warm!

21

Boom, crack! A thunderstorm!

Thunderstorms bring strong winds, heavy rain, booming thunder, and bolts of big lightning. Thunderclouds are really big and tall, and they can make everything go dark—even in the middle of the day.

The air inside a thundercloud moves water droplets up and down. At the top of the cloud, they are ice, but at the bottom they are liquid. When they meet in the middle, they rub together and this creates lightning.

You can use thunder and lightning to work out how far away a thunderstorm is. As soon as you see the lightning, start counting the seconds until you hear the thunder. The sound of thunder takes about five seconds to travel one mile (1.6 kilometers). So divide the number of seconds by five, and you'll know how many miles are between you and the lightning. For instance, a count of 10 seconds means the storm is two miles (three kilometers) away!

Thunderclouds are called cumulonimbus clouds.

When lightning heats up the air, it causes thunder.

Thunderstorms can be exciting, but they are also dangerous, so it's important to know how to stay safe in one.

Don't shelter under trees.

Their height attracts lightning.

Don't use electrical appliances—you might

get a nasty electric shock.

Stay indoors—

heavy winds can flip cars over and uproot trees.

Avoid using water

at home—lightning can travel through plumbing.

Thunderstorms can be big, but they aren't the biggest kind of storm. Tropical cyclones (also called hurricanes or typhoons) are gigantic, rotating storms of howling wind and rain that are extremely dangerous. The wind alone can be strong enough to rip up trees and destroy buildings.

As the swirling warm air rises, the water vapor in it cools and turns into liquid water droplets. These create lots of storm clouds.

Warm, moist air rises over the ocean and is replaced by cooler air. Then the cooler air warms up and rises. The cycle continues over and over.

Tropical cyclones start life over the ocean in tropical regions. These are places that are close to the equator, where the water is always warm.

The wind and clouds begin rotating really fast.

When the wind speed reaches 75 miles per hour (120 kilometers per hour), the storm is now a tropical cyclone. The hole in the center is called the eye.

25

Through the fog

How do you feel about fog? Some people think it looks beautiful, but others think it's pretty creepy. On a foggy day, it can be hard to see very far in front of you.

There are different types of fog. Ground fog happens when there are clear skies and light winds and there is moist air close to the ground. When heat rises on a cloudless night, the ground cools very quickly. Water vapor in the air just above the ground turns into liquid droplets that create fog.

Fog is made of liquid water droplets floating in the air close to the ground. In other words, fog is a kind of low-lying cloud!

Thick fog can reduce visibility to under 3,300 feet (1 kilometer). This is why fog sometimes delays flights—the pilots can't see far enough ahead to land their airplanes.

Be careful in fog—it's easy to get lost.

Sometimes, fog forms very suddenly and disappears really quickly. This is called flash fog. Blink and you'll miss it!

In a foggy valley, sometimes only the tops of mountains are visible.

When cool air sinks down mountains, it pools in valleys. This creates valley fog.

Another type of fog happens when warm, moist air blows over the cold surface of a lake. The water cools the warm air and creates a blanket of fog on the lake.

27

Winter is here. Look out for the snow!

Winter weather is cold, cloudy, and damp. Winter occurs when an area on Earth is farthest from the Sun. The Sun's heat and rays are weaker, daylight is shorter, and the nights are long and cold. It's cloudier too. Sometimes ice crystals fall from the clouds as white, fluffy flakes called snow.

Some trees, called deciduous trees, lose their leaves in winter. This is clever as the leaves need a lot of water-which their trees are unable to get from the cold, frozen soil in winter.

If it's below 32°F (0°C) in a cloud, water vapor freezes into tiny ice crystals. More bits of ice join to make a six-sided pattern—a snowflake. In a big cloud, millions of snowflakes form every second, yet none of them looks the same!

Snow clouds are low and usually pale gray.

The greater the thickness of the ice crystals and size of the water droplets, the deeper the color of the clouds.

Snow is like a white blanket. It works like a blanket, too, keeping things underneath it slightly warmer. No wonder plants start growing beneath! A thick snow blanket is also important for watering the soil. As it slowly melts, a steady stream makes its way down to the roots of the trees, which helps sustain them during dry summers!

Slushy, crunchy, powdery, crusty … In snowy places, people have many words to describe snow. People in Scotland have more than 400!

29

Snow can be lots of fun. We make snowballs, snow people, and snow animals. The tallest snow person ever made stood at almost 130 feet (40 meters).

The world's snowiest place is Japan. In some cities there, more than 50 feet (15 meters) of snow falls each winter. High up on the nearby mountains, it can be twice as snowy.

People who live in snowy places keep snow chains in their vehicles. Once these are attached to the tires, they have more grip.

Snow blocks roads, railroads, and runways. Big, heavy, powerful snowploughs can push it out of the way.

Every 10 minutes, enough snow falls around the world for everyone to make a snow person.

One snowball is made up of about 10,000 flakes, and there are about one million in a snow person.

The weather changes, snow clouds disappear, the Sun comes out, and the snow melts into water. But if this happens too quickly, it may cause another winter problem—floods. The worst floods from melting snow can be more than 50 feet (15 meters) deep. Luckily, most aren't that bad, but rushing streams and rivers can overflow onto fields and roads.

Snow takes up more space than water.

Snow that is 4 inches (10 centimeters) deep melts into water that is 0.4 inches (1 centimeter) deep, but that's a lot of water if it happens in an hour or two!

When the temperature drops below 32°F (0°C), water freezes. Ice is lighter than water, which is why it doesn't sink to the bottom of a frozen lake. Even when ice on a lake is really thick, the water underneath stays liquid. That's good news for the fish, but stepping on the ice can be very dangerous for humans.

Winter is tough for many animals. Some species, like grizzly bears, cope by going to sleep until the spring—this is called hibernation. Others, like this wolf, grow a very thick coat of fur. We all have to keep warm in the winter!

Lake ice might look strong, but it can be very fragile and break easily.

Winter can make it hard for animals to find food.

Chipmunks sleep through most of the winter, too.

Thick gloves are essential when you're on the mountain.

Good boots will stop you slipping on the ice.

The higher up you go, the colder and snowier the weather gets. That's why it's always winter on the tallest mountain in the world: Mount Everest. As well as being permanently chilly up there, it's also harder to breathe because there is less oxygen in the air.

The Sun is stronger at higher altitudes. When it shines on the snow, it can cause snow blindness. Special goggles make it easier to see in these conditions.

Mountaineers carry big knapsacks and camp on the mountainside.

35

Temperatures are rising

When the season changes from winter to spring, it naturally gets warmer. But scientists who study the climate have found that the temperatures on Earth have been rising much too quickly over the past few centuries—this is mostly caused by the things we humans have been doing. The rising temperatures are changing the climate all over the world, and this is changing the weather.

Are weather and climate two different things? Yes, and as we learned, weather is something that can change every day. Climate is a region's typical weather measured over a long period of time—usually 30 years.

An example of climate change is when a dry region becomes wetter over many years. But how did the climate change we are facing today come about?

More and more people are living on the planet and everybody wants to stay warm, cook food, and use electricity! Starting about 200 years ago, we began burning lots of coal, oil, and gas to power things like factories and steam trains. Then came cars, airplanes, and heating for our homes.

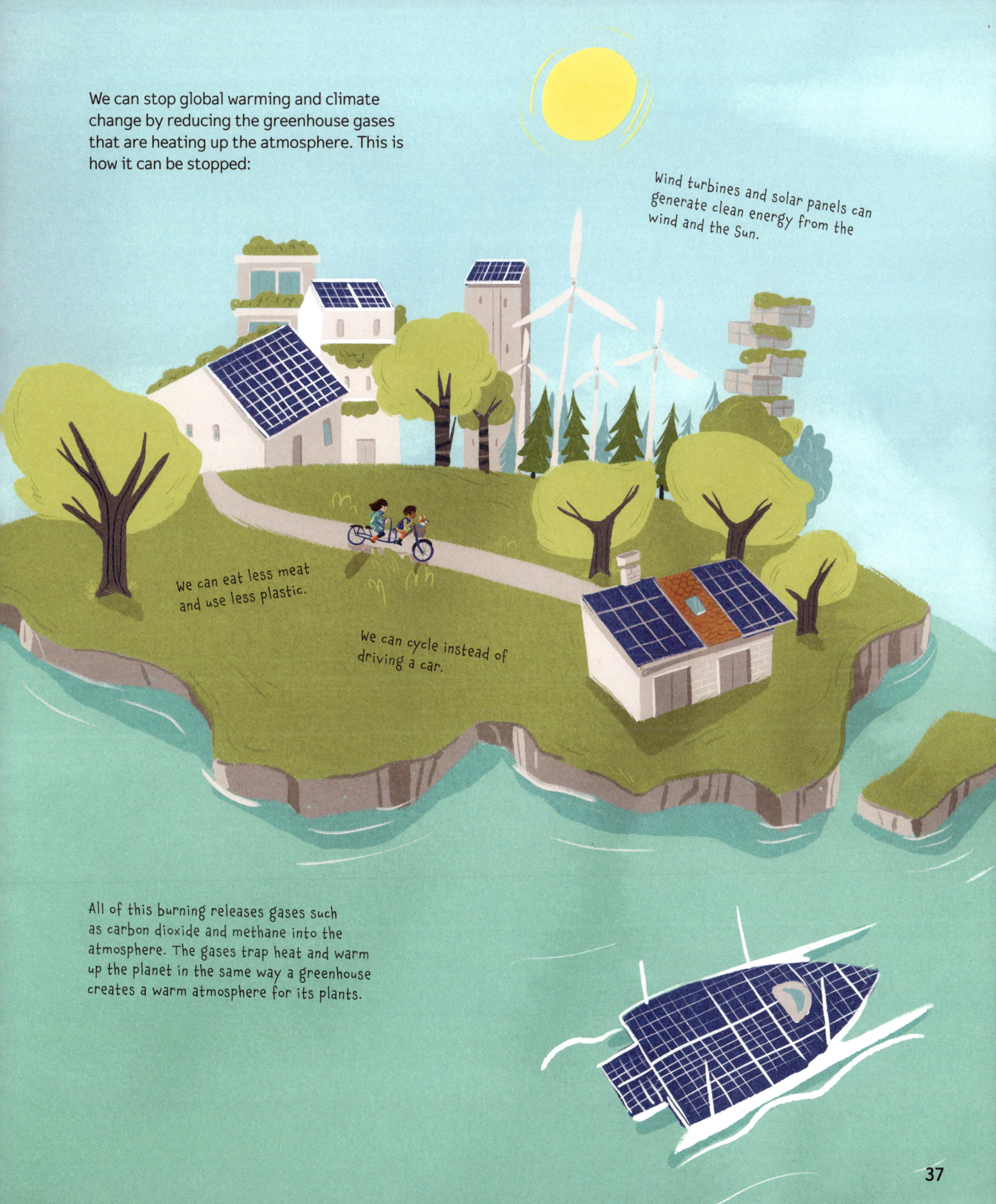

We can stop global warming and climate change by reducing the greenhouse gases that are heating up the atmosphere. This is how it can be stopped:

Wind turbines and solar panels can generate clean energy from the wind and the Sun.

We can eat less meat and use less plastic.

We can cycle instead of driving a car.

All of this burning releases gases such as carbon dioxide and methane into the atmosphere. The gases trap heat and warm up the planet in the same way a greenhouse creates a warm atmosphere for its plants.

Spring is a season of showers

Cirrus clouds are made of ice crystals and look like wispy bits of cotton candy.

They can usually be found above 20,000 feet (6,000 meters).

And showers come from clouds! Clouds can be fat and fluffy, or wispy and flat. Sometimes they even look like funny animals or big dragons. But what are clouds actually made of?

Clouds are tiny water droplets or ice crystals floating in the sky. They are created when warm air rises and then cools in the cold sky. When the droplets or crystals get together in a group, a cloud is formed.

Traveling in an airplane is a great way to see clouds—but the fuel emissions from airplanes help to cause climate change, so we should try to keep air travel to a minimum.

Cumulus clouds look like puffy cotton balls. They float at about 6,500 feet (2,000 meters) or lower.

Clouds aren't always white. The color of a cloud can tell you about the weather, the time of day, or the air quality.

Pinks, purples, and yellows at sunset.

Gray when it rains.

Orange when there's pollution.

Green before a heavy storm.

Other planets in the solar system also have clouds. The clouds on Mars are quite similar to ours, but the ones on Venus are made of sulfuric acid!

Like this hot-air balloon, clouds float because warm air pushes them up from below.

You can't see much inside a cloud, so how do birds fly through them without getting lost? It's thought they can sense where the horizon is, and they can also detect the Earth's natural magnetism, so they keep flying in the right direction.

Without clouds, life on Earth would be difficult. Clouds protect us from the Sun's rays during the day and stop us from getting too cold at night. They also provide the rain that keeps plants and animals alive.

Some clouds grow so tall that it would take you 40 minutes to travel from the bottom to the top of them in an elevator!

Cooling down, the water vapor turns into liquid droplets that form clouds.

When the droplets get too big and heavy to stay in the clouds, they fall to the earth as rain.

Have you ever noticed how it often smells really nice and earthy after it's rained? That smell actually has a name: petrichor. When rain falls onto dry soil, it creates air bubbles that contain the scent. When the bubbles pop, they release the fragrance into the air!

Rainwater flows down mountains ...

... and into the ground.

Water is extremely important. Without it, there would be no life on Earth. Water moves around the Earth and the atmosphere in a never-ending journey called the water cycle.

Rain is one part of the water cycle. We often think that rain is annoying because it stops us from doing fun stuff outdoors. In fact, it's doing us a favor because we need water to survive. Also, squishing through mud after it's been raining is super-fun!

The water vapor rises into the air. High up in the sky, it cools.

They release some of that water into the air as water vapor.

Heat from the Sun turns ocean water into water vapor.

Plants and trees suck up water from the ground.

Have you ever seen a rainbow?

Rainbows are awesome, colorful arcs in the sky. They look real, but they are actually an optical illusion. As it rains, the air is full of water droplets. If the sun shines on these droplets, a rainbow will appear.

To see a rainbow, you have to be standing with the Sun behind you.

Light is made up of many colors. When sunlight travels from the air into a water droplet, it slows down and bends. The bending separates the colors and makes them visible.

Each color bends a little differently. This is why the colors in a rainbow always appear in the same order: red, orange, yellow, green, blue, indigo, violet.

Without rain, we wouldn't have rainbows!

Have you ever tried to find the end of a rainbow? It's impossible! A rainbow will always be the same distance away from you, no matter how fast you run toward it!

Some rainbows are actually complete circles. You have to be really high up to see the whole thing, though.

45

Weather stations can be anywhere. This one is on a hill, but you can also find them in canyons and caves, or on bridges and skyscrapers!

This is a solar panel! It provides the weather station with electricity so that it can record all the information produced by the instruments.

Will it be sunny tomorrow?

Check the forecast! Weather forecasts are important. They help us plan our day-to-day lives—and they help farmers know when to plant crops so that we all have plenty of food. They also keep us safe by letting us prepare for dangerous weather before it arrives.

Forecasting (or predicting) the weather is a skilled job. The scientists who do this are called meteorologists.

Meteorologists use weather stations to monitor what is happening in the atmosphere. The stations contain lots of instruments that help the scientists work out what weather is coming.

An anemometer measures wind speed.

Here's that barometer we first saw a few pages back. Do you remember what it does?

Hygrometers measure the amount of water vapor in the air.

How did people predict the weather before all those instruments were invented?

One way they did it was by watching animals: they believed that animals behaved differently when certain kinds of weather were on the way.

Did you know that crickets chirp faster in warm weather and slower in cold weather? They can even help you calculate the temperature. Just count how many times a cricket chirps in 14 seconds, add 40, and you will have a rough idea of the temperature in Fahrenheit!

Bees and butterflies might also be able to detect changes in air pressure. They don't like the rain, so if they sense that it's coming, they will hide.

The low pressure that causes rain and storms makes it harder for birds to fly high.

Birds flying close to the ground might mean a storm is on the way.

Frogs like to hang out by lakes and croak the night away.

If you hear those croaks getting louder and longer, it could be a sign of rain.

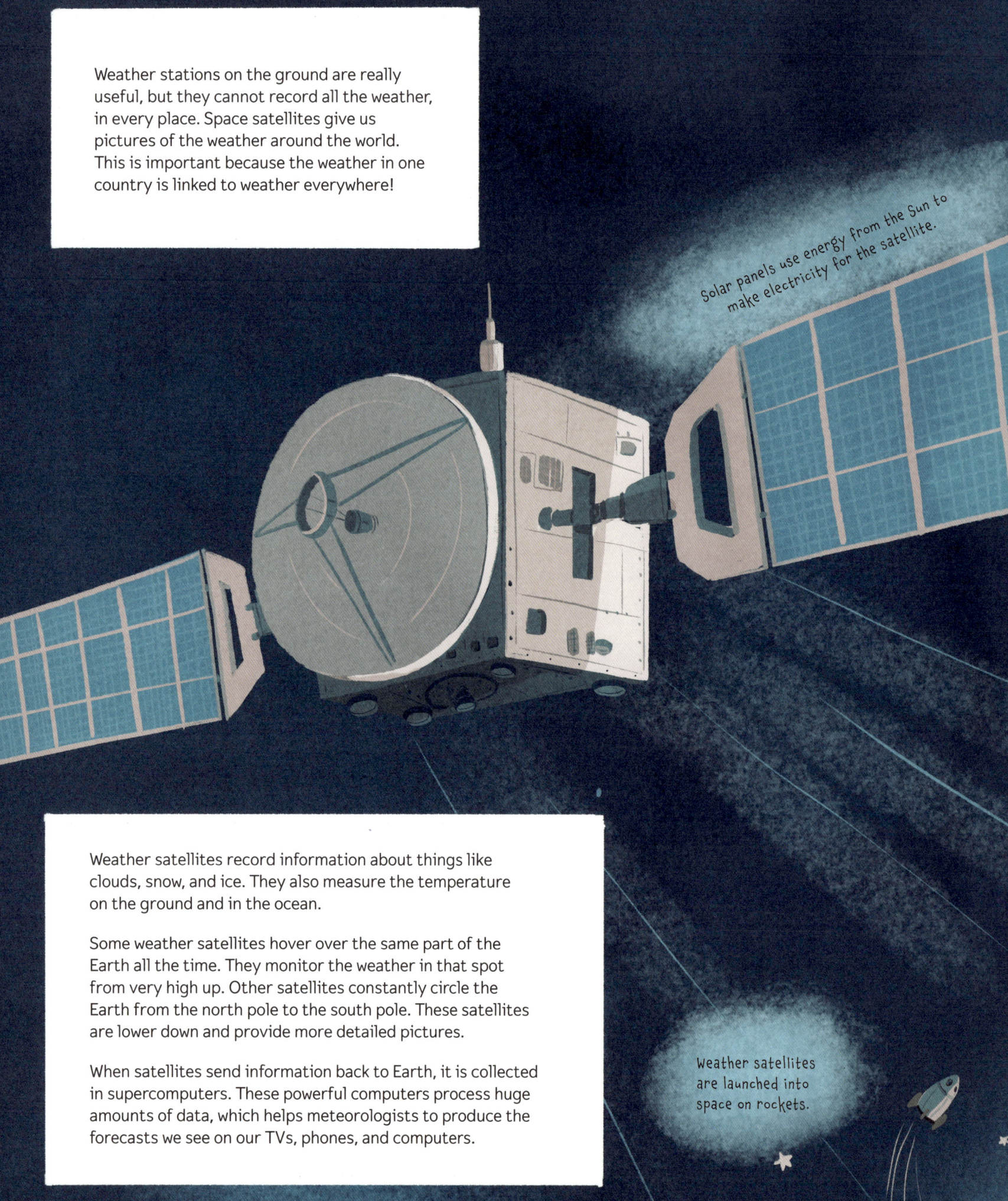

Weather stations on the ground are really useful, but they cannot record all the weather, in every place. Space satellites give us pictures of the weather around the world. This is important because the weather in one country is linked to weather everywhere!

Solar panels use energy from the Sun to make electricity for the satellite.

Weather satellites record information about things like clouds, snow, and ice. They also measure the temperature on the ground and in the ocean.

Some weather satellites hover over the same part of the Earth all the time. They monitor the weather in that spot from very high up. Other satellites constantly circle the Earth from the north pole to the south pole. These satellites are lower down and provide more detailed pictures.

When satellites send information back to Earth, it is collected in supercomputers. These powerful computers process huge amounts of data, which helps meteorologists to produce the forecasts we see on our TVs, phones, and computers.

Weather satellites are launched into space on rockets.

Satellites monitor clouds to tell us ...

... if we can expect storms or clear skies.

The lowest weather satellites are roughly 520 miles (837 kilometers) above the Earth.

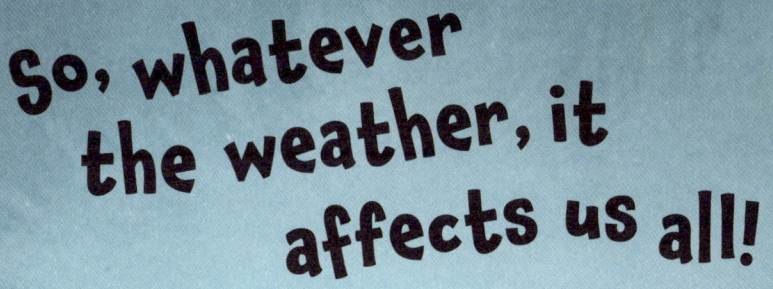

So, whatever the weather, it affects us all!

Wow, you've just learned a whole lot about the weather! Now you know what clouds are, how hurricanes form, and why rainbows are so colorful.

You also know that weather is everywhere. A rainstorm doesn't stop just because it reaches the end of a country. The Sun shines across borders. This means that the weather affects our lives no matter where we are in the world.

And you learned that humans are causing climate change. What will happen in the future? Will there be more extreme weather events? That depends on all of us. If we take care of the world, we will still be able to enjoy sunny summers, windblown leaves in the fall, snowy winter days, and showers and flowers in spring!

Glossary

Anticlockwise: motion in the opposite direction to the hands of a clock

At altitude: high up.

Atmosphere: a layer of gases that surrounds the Earth-otherwise known as air!

Carbon dioxide: one of the gases in our atmosphere. Also a greenhouse gas.

Clockwise: motion in the same direction as the hands of a clock.

Continent: A huge area of land, sometimes separated from other continents by water. The Earth has seven of them.

Drought: when it doesn't rain for a really long time.

Equator: an imaginary line that runs around the center of the Earth, dividing it in half.

Extreme weather: weather that is much more dangerous and destructive than normal weather.

Fahrenheit: a measure of temperature. We write it like this: 70°F

Flood: when an area of dry land becomes submerged under water.

Greenhouse gases: gases that trap heat in our atmosphere, like a greenhouse traps heat for growing tomatoes.

Heat wave: when it stays really hot for a very long time.

High-pressure area: an area with a mass of dry and cool air. It clears the sky, bringing warm weather and sunny skies.

Horizon: the line way off in the distance where it looks like the Earth meets the sky.

kilometers per hour: a measure of speed

Low-pressure area: an area with a mass of moist and warm air. It brings clouds, rainy and windy weather, and even storms.

Magnetic field: a kind of force field. The one we talk about in this book surrounds and protects our planet.

Methane: one of the gases in our atmosphere. Also a greenhouse gas.

miles per hour: a measure of speed

North pole: the northernmost point of the Earth-the very top of the world!

Northern hemisphere: the part of the Earth that is above the equator.

Optical illusion: something that tricks your eyes. What you think you see is different to what is actually there.

Satellite: a machine that is sent into space to travel around the Earth and monitor or communicate things.

Solar panels: panels made of a special material that transforms sunlight into electricity.

Solar system: the system of eight planets (along with lots of stars and moons) that orbit the Sun.

South pole: the southernmost point of Earth-the very bottom of the world!

Southern hemisphere: the part of the Earth that is below the equator.

Sulfuric acid: a strong acid that contains sulfur.

Water vapor: water in the form of gas. When water gets hotter than 212°F (100°C), it turns into vapor.

Wind turbines: very tall, thin windmills. When the wind turns the blades, they generate electricity.

Whatever the Weather

Learn about the Sun, Wind and Rain

Written by Steve Parker and Jen Metcalf

Illustrated by Caroline Attia

This book was conceived, edited, and designed by Little Gestalten.

Edited by Robert Klanten and Maria-Elisabeth Niebius

Design and layout by Emily Sear

Typefaces: Chaloops by Chank Diesel, Hellschreiber by Jörg Schmitt, and KG Miss Kindergarten by Kimberly Geswein

Printed by Schleunungdruck GmbH, Marktheidenfeld

Made in Germany

Published by Little Gestalten, Berlin, 2021

ISBN 978-3-96704-711-0

For more information, and to order books, please visit www.little.gestalten.com.

Bibliographic information published by the Deutsche Nationalbibliothek.

The Deutsche Nationalbibliothek lists this publication in the Deutsche Nationalbibliografie; detailed bibliographic data are available online at www.dnb.de.

This book was printed on paper certified according to the standards of the FSC®.